Turn Your 'Jo My Son

Our Blessed Mother's Poetry

As Recorded by
Rose T. Holland

8-7-99
Don II,
Stand up
proud as
you show
Our Lord
your love-
Love-
Rose

COVER DESIGN:	H. Donald Kroitzsh
ILLUSTRATIONS:	Rose T. Holland
INTRODUCTION:	Rose T. Holland
FOREWORD:	Father Daniel A. Torres
POETRY:	Our Blessed Mother
EDITING & LAYOUT:	H. Donald Kroitzsh

For information or orders contact:
Five Corners Publications, 5052 Route 100, Plymouth, Vermont 05056, USA
phone — 802-672-3868 or
Rose T. Holland, P O Box 1396, Lake Charles, LA 70602, USA
phone (toll free) — 877-551-8138, FAX 318-562-2738

Printed and bound in Canada

Published by:
Five Corners Publications, Ltd.
5052 Route 100
Plymouth, Vermont 05056
USA

Turn Your Face To My Son
ISBN 1-886699-19-4

To my husband, Bob Holland,
and
my three children, Laurel, Beau, and Bobby

Special Thanks

To God the Father, the Son, and the Holy Spirit.

To Our Blessed Mother

To my husband, Bob Holland, for growing with me on our spiritual journey, and for his love, affirmation, and encouragement.

To my three children, Laurel, Beau, and Bobby, for listening, loving, believing, and following Christ.

To my parents, John and Camille Timpa, for all they gave to me from their hearts.

To my great grandmother and grandmother, Caterina Pitarra and Sarah Pitarra, for their legacy of faith.

To my spiritual director, Father Danny Torres, for his guidance, commitment to God, and teachings of perseverance.

To my rosary group and adoration prayer group for listening to the messages and poems each week and for their friendship in Christ:
Cathy L. Martin, Tina Deshotel, Leisa Henry, Judy Rosteet, Ira Belle Adrian, Camille Timpa (Mom), Libby Timpa, Kitty Eccles, Gwen Burguieres, Cheryl LeBlanc, Evelyn Ardoin, Judy Doucet, Elaine Heape, Maria Jones, Susan Hebert, Martha Reasonover, Mary Becker, Helen Simon.

To the St. Theresa Community, Lay Carmelites (Third Order) for being zealous for the Lord as disciplines of faith, hope, and love.

INTRODUCING TURN YOUR FACE TO MY SON

Almost ten years ago, on June 23,1988, my husband and I went on a pilgrimage to Medjugorje, Yugoslavia. Visiting this site, where the Blessed Virgin Mary began appearing in 1981 to six children, led to incredible events. Many petitions were answered, and of course, our lives have never been the same. As for most pilgrims returning from this holy place, there is a strong desire to discover what God is calling us to do. This was only the beginning of our conversion. Soon after our return, my husband became a Catholic, and I was commissioned to be a Lay Minister of the Holy Eucharist, a gift that I dearly cherish. We joined the family choir at our church, began weekly perpetual adoration of the Holy Eucharist, and in 1993, we each made a Catholic Cursillo—a walk with Jesus. I began attending rosary group every Wednesday, and we had our home Enthroned to the Sacred Heart of Jesus. This is an old Catholic traditional ceremony when a family pronounces Jesus as head of their hearts and home. Although my spiritual growth was enhanced, and my conversion had deepened, I knew that God was not finished with me.

We were continuing to live our faith, when another experience changed my life even further, and subsequently changed that of my family and friends as well. On June 25, 1993, I began receiving inner locutions from Our Lord. At that time I had never heard of this term. An inner locution is an interior voice that is heard, and one's own mind is not used. It is not possible for me to completely comprehend what occurs; I only know that I become the pen of the writer, and the writer is Our Lord. I believe that this is a gift of the Holy Spirit because of the many graces we have continued to receive. Spiritual direction has accompanied and intensified my numerous religious endeavors. Although our primary vocation is being parents to our three wonderful children, my husband and I have embraced a second vocation in the Lay Carmelites (Third Order). On June 23, 1997, we journeyed on a pilgrimage to the Holy Land led by my spiritual director, Father Daniel A. Torres. This was a spirit-filled event that brought to life the word of God. An account of my journey, Our Lord's messages, and incidents ramified through these messages, from 1993 to the present date, will be included in my next book entitled, *Journey of Faith*.

Our Lord has asked that I now share with you words from His Mother, which I began receiving in 1996 through inner locutions. The Blessed Virgin Mary began conferring to me a series of messages for the youth, and then she began reciting poetry. Sometimes, she will relate a message prior to a poem, but she often presents a poem exclusively. In her closing, she often refers to herself as *Gospa*, which means "Our Lady" in Croatian. Messages from Our Lord and the Blessed Mother are received weekly and at various significant times. They are received only while in meditation and prayer, and usually during my adoration hour. These messages and poems are written within 5 to 10 minutes. After you read them, you will know in your heart that I am not the author. I believe that God asked me to be a vessel, and my only true contribution is saying yes.

Turn Your Face to My Son is comprised of Our Lady's poetry, an extraordinary way in which we are once again being called to her Son. Her expressions and thoughts will take you back in a way that will necessitate meditation, reflection, and examination of your spiritual life. It was not until I began typing the collection that I realized how Our Lady gives themes throughout her vibrant words. Although she has given many messages and apparitions throughout the world, to my knowledge, there is no other collection of poetry from her. The book is set up chronologically and includes only her poetry. The bolded statements either came from a message prior to a poem or from a significant message in the poem. I believe that this book can be facilitated in a number of ways, perhaps for daily reading or for meditation.

My hope is that you, the reader, regardless of the status of your journey, catch a glimpse of this mysterious encounter through her words. I pray that each of you can open your heart to God's love, and find the one goal that we all should have in this life—the salvation of souls. Through listening to God, your soul will receive a special grace, enriched by His light. God sent His only Son to us for our salvation, and now He has sent His Mother to us for conversion of our souls and in preparation for His coming.

Rose T. Holland
Lake Charles, Lousiana

FOREWORD

~ *Fr. Daniel A. Torres* ~

The ultimate goal of life is being with God. For each of us, we experience God uniquely, as Father, Son, Spirit, Lover, and Creator. We realize that relationship is Love. From what we receive — the gift of Love — we are called to become images of Love for one another.

We all have different gifts in bringing God's Love to others. For us to know those gifts, we need to spend ample time with our Lord in prayer. Prayer is that relationship with oneself and God. The more that we find in prayer, the more we will discover about the truth of ourselves and the power of God's Love for us.

We must persevere in prayer. Blessed Julian of Norwich, one of the beloved mystics of the Church wrote this:

> "Our prayer brings great joy and gladness to our Lord. He wants it and awaits it.
>
> By His grace He can make us as like Him in inward being as we are in outward form. This is His blessed will.
>
> So He says this, 'pray inwardly, even though you find no joy in it. For it does good, though you feel nothing, see nothing, yes, even though you think you cannot pray. For when you are dry and empty, sick and weak, your prayers please Me, though there be little enough to please you. All believing prayer is precious to me.'
>
> God accepts the goodwill and work of His servants, no matter how we feel.
>
> It pleases God that by the help of His grace we should work away at our praying and our living, directing all our powers to Him until in the fullness of joy we have Him whom we seek — Jesus."

ENDNOTE:
LLEWELYN, ROBERT EDITED: *THE JOY OF THE SAINTS SPIRITUAL READINGS THROUGHOUT THE YEAR* TEMPLEGATE PUBLISHERS, SPRINGFIELD, ILLINOIS 1989, PAGE 41.

"In cases which concern private revelations, it is better to believe than not to believe, for if you believe, and it is proven true, you will be happy that you believed, because our Holy Mother asked it. If you believe, and it should be proven false, you will receive blessings as if it had been true, because you believed it to be true."

His Holiness, Pope Urban VIII, 1623-44

Turn Your Face

to My Son

"You shall love the Lord, your God,
with all your strength, and with all your
mind, and your neighbor as yourself."

Luke 10:27

...I stand beside my Son, and I ask for your love and goodness. I ask my little children to follow me so that I can lead them to my Son. He has sent me to teach you to pray and show you the direction that you must follow...

Do not follow others,
For they may not know the way.
Lead and know of the direction,
And you will not stray.

Pray and know the meaning,
For it's deep inside your hearts.
Speak with love and kindness,
And there our hearts won't part.

Stay awhile and ponder,
On the love our God has lost.
Guide, it is your mission;
Don't hide, there is a cost.

Compassion, is still awaiting,
For those who find a way.
Love, it is the answer,
For each of you today.

With tears of sorrow,
Your Loving Gospa

...One child that follows the flock will be many when Our grace is opened to all of you...

One child of grace saved, is one child that will pray.
One child that prays, brings many more Our way.
Sing to the mountains, sing to the stars.
From the glory of heaven, your gifts are Ours.

Your Heavenly Mother

...The saints fought the
battle of invading imperfection...

A prayer in silence, or a prayer aloud.
Show my Son your love, as you stand up proud.
Show the sinners the glory that's at your side.
Maybe the story will conquer the tide.

Your Loving Gospa

...Know that the
"Fire of Love" within will guide you
in the indiscernible days that are ahead...

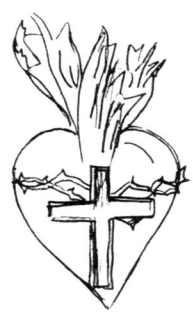

Blessed are those who follow Us today.
Blessed are their hearts.
I pray.

Pure and serene, may their spirits unfold.
Many are loved, many remain.
Steadfast to all, that my Son can hold.

Your Loving Gospa
Crowned with Glory

...Join in my Son's passion,
and this Unity of Sacrifice
will show your willingness to serve Him...

Prepare and know that We are near.
Practice all the prayers and not fear.
We walk beside Our faithful loved.
We send the storm, We'll send the dove.

Your Loving Gospa

...Recognize, believe, and say "yes"
to the Glory that is yours today...

See the veil and see the glory.
Say the prayer, tell the story.
It takes your arms to join with mine.
It's saying "yes" to the grace that's divine.

Many a foe will pass this by.
My angels of youth will raise you high.
It's trusting your Lord, my Son, my Love.
It's seeing His face, come down from above.

So scurry, my ones, don't linger in doubt.
Your faith, hope, and love, that's what it's about.
Praependo my Son, Praependo awhile.
They're gathering sheep, they're learning to smile.

Your Loving Gospa
Crowned with Glory

Praependo means "hang" in Latin.

Peace is flowing like a river through my
loved ones who are following me to my Son...

Today we pray for souls that are weak.
Tomorrow the search, for Christ we will seek.

Pray my ones, pray with your heart.
Pray for the soldiers, you are in the dark.

Light will become your stream to follow.
Sparing the meek, filling the shallow.

Send them your love as I send you mine.
Search for Our Lord, for His Mercy's Divine.

A rose I will send you, its fragrance so sweet.
The grace, it will greet you the day that we meet.

Your Loving Mother

**My Son has called you,
and you have answered Him...**

The love you give is given this day.
It's given to those who don't even pray.
The faith that you show brings example and strength.
The joy that you share is a gift that is sent.

Hope brings us faith, it strengthens tomorrow.
Only those without it will see its great sorrow.
See the Great Light, its glimmer so small.
Know that its glory awaits those who call.

As you stand in the sun and feel the heat of Our love.
The strength to endure will grace you from above.
Send up your sorrow, pray for awhile.
The wind of your love, the wind of your smile.

Your Loving Mother

...The glow of sanctity
will surround you as you choose
this aspiring condition of soul and grace...

Behold, my Son awaits His flock.
Behold, please give your heart within.
The choice is love, not anger or sin.
Behold, my Son rejects all the mock.
Open your heart, Grace will unlock.

Can you not hang for the Grace Divine?

Behold, I should go to awaken the rest.
The furry they see brings but a test.
Behold the cup, that brings forth a glow.
This is the life within you will know.

Pray all my children, pray it's been time.
Break this great bread, taste the great wine.
Know it takes courage to give all you have.
It takes less than a thought to follow Our path.

Behold, it's a prayer given each day.
To reflect in Our grace, to see a great face.
And to know that your light is directed this way.
To know that your heart beams a ray as you pray.

Your Loving Gospa

...My little ones, work for my Son,
and peace will work in your life...

Prepare the Way of the Lord, my ones be kind.
Prepare your hearts with praise you find.
Know that a gift awaits within.
Know that my Son to you I send.

Seek to know Him, grace is yours too.
Seek to find a friend, He is calling you.
Sow the seed Our Lord extends.
Plant this seed and grow to no end.

And as your gifts of peace flourish through,
You'll see the glory, and know it's true.
Hang not your heads in sadness and gloom.
Hang only in Honor of the Son you'll see soon.

Praise His presence, before you with love.
Praise His presence, it's here from above.
Empty your soul to the One in the light.
He will lift up your spirit, He will take you in flight.

Sing to the mountains, let your heart soar.
Giving such grace brings light all the more.
Lift up it all to the shades of blue,
And as I wrap arms around you, I'll carry you through.
As I wrap arms around you, you'll feel His love too.

Your Loving Mother

...Seek to know my Son today, so that
you will recognize Him when you see Him...

Know His prayers, know His sorrow.
Live His love, face tomorrow.
Know His heart, with yours be one.
Know Him well, know my Son.

Eyes still opened, eyes still closed.
Know His presence that unfolds.
Let your life be His spirit too.
Let your song be sung, it's for you.

In knowing Him, the best way you know.
You find His presence wherever you go.
And when the mountain top you reach.
Not a word to recall or even a speech.

You'll feel His glory, you'll see His face too.
You'll know that His truth was lived by you.
You'll know that His love led your love through.
To live in His glory and know it is true.

Your Heavenly Mother

…May the rocks below your feet
allow you to embrace my Son's love
as you step in His shoes and walk His path…

May His grace be ever at your side.
Above, below, in strength, in stride.

May your hearts extend to reach its peak.
To feel His presence, to hear Him speak.

And lowly does your journey begin.
Each new dawning, each new end.

Abide in His love, continue at best.
Take only the graces, take only a rest.

For in finding His resting place and facing the sun.
You'll find His great glory, you'll know you're the one.

Extend your hearts to praise His name.
Reach for the stars, feel His great pain.

Reach for the stars, praise is your name.
Reach for the stars, His glory you'll gain.

Your Mother of Love

...A child has been born into my arms...

A child has been born into my arms.
Swaddled in cloth, protected from harm.
The light in His eyes glistens so bright.
My child, He was born in a manger this night.

The angels are singing in glory and praise.
Holy His Name, glowing His face.
The joy that He brings to all of the land.
The praise we must give with the touch of our hand.

Holy is this night, blessed in love.
Holy is this site, adorned from above.
Blessed this gift, Lord, You did bring.
Joseph, my love, He has sent us a King.

Your Blessed Mother

This message was received while in the Holy Land,
at the site of the Nativity.

...My children, to live the prayer
in your lives is now the true journey...

Prepare the road, it's now your feat.
To show the peace to each you meet.

To find the love, its weight is gold.
To know the journey your life beholds.

Nurture those, whom you they will follow.
Find in your ways to fill hearts that are hollow.

Shine forth the life, my Son's truth you know.
Shine forth the peace, the light from His glow.

Know that the riches, not silver, not gold.
Are found in the hearts of the young and the old.

Of the people who live, God only their strength.
Not measured by pounds, not measured in length.

The gift of pure heart, it's the richest by far.
If it's filled with God's glory, if it's protected in war.

For the "poorest in spirit" will be remembered in prayer.
Not from their lack of, not from their despair,

But from the peace and the love that shines from within.
From the gold in their hearts, from the <u>faith</u> that He sends.

Your Loving Mother

...you must spread this peace among
His people like a blanket over the cold...

The peace you find will take the curve.
Get you through, help you serve.
The love you give will get you through,
The hardened hearts, the chosen few.

Recall the love He suffered for.
Recall the place you traveled afar.
Feel the spirit, feel the hope.
Open your hearts, let go of the rope.

Faith will grow, it's the flower's dirt.
Injury pardoned, taking pain from the hurt.
Open the wings my Son to you sent.
Fly like His birds with peace that is meant.

Take hold of their hands, you now know the way.
You can teach them to live, you can teach them to pray.
For with this giving of love the river will flow.
And the faith, hope, and love will continue to grow.
Bring back all this love to the land that you know.

Your Loving Mother

...Prayer is a continual desire
for Christ and a continual examination
of faith, and of mind, body, and soul...

Prepare your heart, prepare in love.
My Son is waiting for this love above.
He seeks to find you at the foot of His cross.
Desiring His love, not finding a loss.

To seek beyond, the meadow's clear.
To find perfection without fear.
To know your searching's not in vain.
For prayer will carry you from pain.

My Son is pleased for those who endure.
The love you show to all is pure.
Prepare your hearts each day with care.
Know We love to answer prayer.

Seek to find, the way will unfold.
The faith you know will keep you bold.
The charity that's given free to all.
Will bring desire, to practice in your call.

Love, my friends, it's your heart's only desire.
To have the peace, to feel joy transpire.
The way to all is at your door—
The heart that loves my Son, evermore.

Your Loving Gospa

...I have come to plead for your conversions and love, and many follow my Son...

Pray my child,
Pray to no end.
The depth of your love,
To you We send.

In times you will suffer.
In time you will rejoice.
The soul of such longing,
Will lend you such choice.

Be sure, be bold,
For intensity will exist.
Know We are with you.
Know faith will persist.

Envelop such love.
Take only the gold.
Into your pure hearts,
The truth He'll behold.

Your Mother, Your Love

...The army of love,
that you have become, will be
the rainbow that extends peace and love,
and wins the battle that presides amongst all...

To love thy neighbor to no end,
Is such a task, for they aren't a friend.
But find a special spot in your heart.
The prayer you say, it is a start.

Some are stale, some need <u>new skins</u>.
The grace God sends, it will begin,
To break down walls and give a call,
To love renewed or faith installed.

You see, my child, this grace He'll give.
A reminding choice, for them to live.
The outcome, only my Son's will.
The Blood of Christ to them you fill.

And if a shepherd they become.
My Lord, my Son, He will have won.
And as you pray remember them.
God gives this choice until the end.

Come forth in silence, only to see,
The servant of Christ you've learned to be.
All won't fulfill requests from grace,
But those who do will see His face.

With tears of sorrow, yet tears of love,
Your Loving Mother from above.

...Stand as I stood, beside my Son,
knowing His destiny, awaiting the sun...

Recall my silence, recall my tears,
Remember the love that calmed my fears.
Stand as I stood, beside my Son,
Knowing His destiny, awaiting the sun.

Walk not in His shadow, but within His skin,
To breathe and act as He did, again, and again.
Be proud of this choice, know trial it will bring.
The tortures of life can't reach hearts that sing.

Alleluia and praise to His name you must live.
Protection and grace to your life He'll give.
So standing on sand with no water to drink,
No thirst will you find, no heart will then sink.

Know love and show virtue of patience and care.
Remember to wait at the cross and prepare.
For the toil and the seasoning, with you is true,
And the grace to withstand is given to you.

With love for Our Lord
from your Father's Hand,
and peace flowing through
your Mother to you—

Your Loving Gospa

...O Star of the Sea, O Star of the Night...

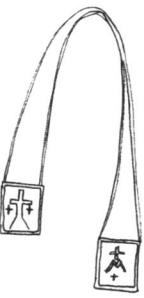

I speak, my children, you have become—
My morning star, my Son's chosen one.
To wear my cloth with pride and gleam.
To show His love, His will Supreme.

Extend your hand, extend your heart.
For joining me, we'll never part.
I'm with your team in all your walks.
I'll shine with grace on all your talks.

Prepare, in spirit, with trust and care.
My Son assists as you prepare.
In doing this work, His Spirit of Peace,
Will take away struggles, concerns will cease.

Endure in this path—the sun, you're its shine.
It's a treasure of presence, this tree and its vine.
Know spirit is true, a prayer, it's a life.
O Star of the Sea, O Star of the Night.

So let those stars guide you, you answered this call.
Indeed, my Son leads me to shield every fall.
For in doing His work, this task thus you know,
You, I take with me wherever I go.

Your Loving Mother—Star of the Sea

The gifts I have given from my Son
are a sign of His everlasting love...

I carry these buds to you today.
Please water them carefully.
Please, take them and pray.
And after they're full,
With a blooming of God's love,
Give them back,
I will hold them at your place up above.

Your Loving Mother

...Know that although the tide
of life seems to cover the shore,
We are here making sure that
your sail is directing toward the sun...

Ever more is the light from within you to see.
Holy His presence, given through me.
Know that the birth of this Son from above,
Has brought a great light, has sent you a dove.

The temple my Son created within.
Is there for your longing, for forgiveness of sin.
Rejoice, you are chosen. Rejoice, thee on high.
Know of God's pleasure, know of His sigh.

In the love you extend to the people you meet,
Find the love from within you, a place they each greet.
Look ahead, look above, look around, look beyond too.
And the grace will be shining, give obedience, and find you.

In the river of peace, you won't sink, you will glide.
For you'll look to the Father, with gleam and with pride.
Turn around and be humble, turn to your friend.
He's my Son, He's your Father, He's the temple within.

Your Loving Gospa

…You must serve first the Lord, and all graces will be yours…

The sun is shining, it leads your way.
The brightened hearts will prepare and stay.

Within His glory, within His grace.
Know of His pain, stand firm in your place.

The grazing is going to set in the fields.
Tell of His story, use love as the shields.

Prepare only your souls, the rest isn't yours.
Encourage the many who struggle for cures.

My child, you are near and the course lighted bright.
You've been through the valleys, you've walked in the night.

So sing of such praise in the face of the sun.
Pray for His children, extending "will be done".

Awaken the hungry, feed only the poor.
Their spirits are rising, their hearts will then soar.

My child, have no fear, for those wars will not cease.
Until peace prevails, this tragedy will increase.

Endure with all strength, endure 'til the end.
My Son suffers kindly, and love still He'll send.

Look to the North, around you, prepare.
It's the sound of the symbols, it's the sound of the snare.

Take care, these souls look for the guidance We give you.
The chosen, not all, will be far and few.

The sun's shining brightly, it's marking your course.
Find only love, faith and joy, my Son as the source.

Within the great castles, built from within.
You'll see the great glory of Sanctity's friend.
You may live this light, for God's love is the end.

Your Woman of Peace
Mother of Sorrow
Guidance and Grace
Today and Tomorrow

...Within your fortress longing,
you build His gleaming throne...

As your guide, I bring the colors of
The wind, the sun, the stars.
With white so pure as heaven,
Shining grace of ever Ours.

Into my light so brightly
Are the depths my Son invites.
Take faith and care abiding to the
Place He brings delights.

Into the sun I take you,
It's not hot, not cold, intense.
Into His castle boldly, do I bring you,
And with Him, you commence.

You bring back the shine within you
Of this everlasting home.
And within your fortress longing,
You build His gleaming throne.

And once you know the arrow of
The peace that must abide,
You plan and go so near it,
To your castle, Christ inside.

Your Mother,
Your Peace,
Grace will not cease.

...And while He hangs awaiting peace,
I come with grace, for war to cease...

The dress I wear is white and blue.
The grace I send is meant for you.
Become the chosen at His feet.
Become the one who is complete.

Enjoy the glow you feel within.
His light, so lasting, until the end.
For in His heart this light is born.
In His suffering did I mourn.

Embrace the grace my Son thus sends.
The purity of heart thus all depends.
On choice, my child, and acting faith too.
On living life with love's only Truth.

Encourage those who seek to find.
The place you've been, that left behind.
And show that sorrow of our King's death.
Live His glory with each living breath.

And while He hangs awaiting peace,
I come with grace, for war to cease.
And gather many through the torch,
Calling souls to purity's parch.

Embrace the love, your longing cry,
Of life for living, death not die.
Prepare and know this gown of blue,
Is gracing all, embracing you.

Gather all and quickly see,
That peace my Son bestows on thee.
And flourish may the ageless soul,
Purity, love, its only goal,
Flourishing the ageless soul.

Your Loving Mother

...Invite me into your homes, so that my conquest will be complete...

Be bold with love, be proud with grace.
Invest in the glory that crowns His face.
Be humble and steadfast, the two do combine.
Prepare in this tarry, partake of His wine.

The longings they search for are right there inside.
The love He did send you, the hope that presides.
The searching, though plenty, has led them thus far.
To seek Thee, to find the gifts of the stars.

To share in the glory of heavenly grace.
Is loving thy neighbor, living this pace.
To join me in prayer, to open your doors,
Brings these gifts that He's bringing, the ones He thus stores.

So love, it's the prayer, salvation the goal.
Heavenly courts await those, this that they hold.
Though seasons may last, their time it has passed.
For the hearts of the faithful and the fire of such love,
Will flourish within you, to last and to last.

Your Loving Mother

...May the roses Our little angel sends,
bring sweetness at each river's bend...

May the roses Our little angel sends,
Bring sweetness at each river's bend,
And delight, the prize of every life,
For peace you find removes your strife.

Behold the Grandeur of Our King.
He gives His Blood for each living thing.
To have and hold with love expressed,
The choice of God, the life of test.

Examine all, partake at best.
The living lamb before your chest.
Exchange the parts of you impure,
In taking Him within to cure.

Before you, does He offer you,
A life eternal, a presence too.
So ask yourself in fairness quest,
Do you choose life or choose the best?

It's now His work, you must withhold,
This life of challenge, place of cold.
So grasp these sweet petals, Our Therese does send,
His love, His Blood, His Heart within.

Your Loving Gospa

...The praise you must give
is the temple you build...

Protect those you love, it's a season so cold.
Be true to your King, there's a story yet told.
Delight in His arms that are stretched for your glory.
Be kind to the foe who has stolen your flurry.
Invest in such care to the ones you do love,
And love given now to the ones with no prairie.
My grace I give as a sign of my presence.
The white of the sun and the rain's deepest hue,
Are giving a cleanse and are sending to you—
The power within you that searches for more,
The sustaining endurance, a heart that will soar.

Your Mother, Your Love

...From thy soul will heaven sing...

The crosses that you carry,
With grace I shower thee.
The windows of your soul,
You open onto thee.

Embrace your King of Glory,
Empowered with all love.
And to you these graces many,
From my Dear Son above.

So the question do you ask,
From my heart, to thee I bring.
And the answer of tomorrow,
From thy soul will heaven sing.

Your Loving Mother

...Grace will be flowing,
for the Spirit is true...

What is grace? The state you are in,
The place you see love, freedom from sin.
The compassion, no fear, the motivating force,
That teaches you patience, hope, love of course.

It's a sparrow in flight, it's the seed that you sow.
It's the glow from within you, that you didn't know.
It's forever a smile, a glance, and a prayer,
For the one you didn't like or the one love you share.

Beyond all the shadows of life that you see,
Grace will bring Glory, bring peace that is free.
Grace will be flowing, for the Spirit is true.
Grace is the love from my Son, through me, to you.

Your Loving Gospa

...Hold your rosaries in your hands...

Hold your rosaries in your hands.
Be prepared for mission's stand.
With the wind I bring the Spirit One.
With the rain, I send the sun.

In the grace, you must be ever,
For its protection ever more.
Don't let fear invoke your glory,
Don't let haste be at your door.

Be with love and peace be with you.
It's the everglade of now.
Be my child, the Christ within you.
Be my love, my Son is proud.

Take the pain and pleasure both.
They're with Will of His they come.
Be the guide, the soul retriever.
Be the saint, believe the One.

Trust in all He sends to mold you.
For the love and care will be
The harps, the notes within you.
The love that sets you free.

Your Loving Mother

...You see of the army, your friends have become...

To "Wednesday's Girls"

Pray with a heart that's open and true.
Pray for a smile from someone who's blue.
Bring them the waves of grace in your smile.
Give them a reason to stay for awhile.

Beyond the horizon the mansions so high,
Are waiting to greet you, to shadow a sigh.
And during your duties as soldier to a King,
You find in your heart the glory He brings.

When finding such truth, the word written one,
You see of the army, your friends have become.
And raising them up to my Son's beaten brow,
You give them a tear, you show them just how.

So gather, reflect, pray, fight defeat.
The sharing of love in your group is unique.
Bring Peace to the world, your mission's not through.
Bring love through your smiles, hold your rosaries, I hold you.

Your Loving Gospa

This poem is addressed to Rose's weekly rosary group.

...The King in my arms
is requesting your strength...

My children, each time you prepare,
And think you are ready,
But this world full of creatures,
Keeps you unsteady.

You're never full proof of the sins that prevail,
And as you protect your heart
You will see, it takes daily work,
From morning to dark.

My children, I ask of your prayer,
And your praise, the King in my arms
Is requesting your strength.
He's asking for love, hearts burning warm.

Examine such hearts and protect,
In your love, the grace He has sent you.
The love you must give,
For the Will of the Father is only that true,
The Will that is His, that will carry you through.

Your Loving Mother

...Our presence We bring,
to wrap you with care, for the giving
of thanks, for the love that We share...

The thanks you must give must be daily, my friend.
The little ways you show that you care and extend.
Family or friends, those unknown to you,
Are worthy of thanks, they're God's gift too.

For peace in a time when peace does not prevail,
Is "just" for a thank you, a welcome, a hail.
And prayer given for those less in the light,
Will surely give thanks for the blessings tonight.

Become one that gives from the heart of so pure.
Be one with Our Father, the "One", rest assure.
And the thanks you can give, a prayer for another,
Will be all so pleasing a gift to your brother.

Bring peace from your presence to others you meet.
Extend only your hand, the heart it will greet.
Our presence We bring, to wrap you with care,
For the giving of thanks, for the love that We share.

Your Loving Gospa

...Let the children live...

The joy I send as new life begins,
Is the answer to prayer, an answer He sends.
May life be your choice for those He creates,
Not hatred or misery or changes in state.

Behold each new blessing, each nativity in life,
The struggling infants, the life with a fight.
Take hold, recognize the sin, it is near.
My children are taking these lives out of fear.

Stand firm in your choice, it's a life just as Christ.
They still crucify Him, still paying the price.
Speak loudly my loved ones, your call can be heard,
For the swaddled I'm holding may speak of God's word.

Let the children live.

Your Mother of the Stars

…My Son in your heart
is your shield that unfolds…

My Son brings such glory to those who will seek
The love of the Father, the prayer for the meek.
Prepare in your way, for these times aren't of Him.
They find pleasure in hurting, in sin in the end.

The angels are guiding those folding their hands.
They're watching Our children, they're over the lands.
Be watchful as ever, the evil that waits,
Looking for weakness, right outside heaven's gates.

Until We return to this world, peace will be
A struggle for many, a war in this sea.
So scurry, my little ones, time it is short.
Don't lose, the unfaithful are wanting your heart.

Be bold in your faith, my Son wants this lead.
He's asking for prayers, for love to exceed.
So take not such armor that you can hold,
My Son in your heart is your shield that unfolds,
The love you must have for the truth to be told.

Your Loving Gospa

...Await with me at the foot of the
cross and seek only His dwelling within...

Our love is with you, Our presence so sure,
We're seeking the loving, We're seeking the pure.

Find vastly the hunger of love, it is life.
Be strong, faith can't falter, it's leading the fight.

My loved ones, hold fast to the lessons you know.
For the sun's morning light won't melt your faith's snow.

Your Loving Gospa

...I gazed to the heavens in
wonder if one day, the King I was
raising would show you to pray...

A mother watches over her children, with a grace from above.
She gives all the glory I send with His love.

She sings of the sparrow that followed by day.
She longs for the Spirit to guide them to stay.

The teachings of love, those white or those gray,
Are given so freely, the babe's on its way.

And as this child grows, not in inches but in strength,
Your love and your kindness within them takes length.

I watched over my Son, in awe as He passed,
Not just through the valley, but through hearts, and they last.

I gazed to the heavens in wonder if one day,
The King I was raising would show you to pray.

The answer for many in the guidance that they give,
Is the faith, hope, and love you have taught them to live.

So gaze in the Sun, and in wonder, as I did.
Know that within them, His heart, they do live.

The kindness and love of a child for its mother
Is the grace from above, shared with each other.

I send them this message, with grace to their heart,
Protection and guidance from heaven won't part.

Those graced from young, with this love from above,
Will become my Son's soldiers in this world needing love.

Your Mother of Peace

...May the peace that I bring you
fill each heart you touch, with a love
that reminds you—He loves you that much...

I speak of His words to pass across your lips,
Love of your brother, peace your heart grips.

Spend time with my Son, His lessons of true.
Give of your heart to a neighbor or two.

Be patient my children, keep gathering sheep.
My children keep sleeping, awake them from sleep.

This time He's allowing is taking the toll.
The weak and unfaithful are losing their souls.

So gather in silence, the echo of love.
My Son hears you loudly, He's watching above.

May the peace that I bring you fill each heart you touch,
With a love that reminds you—He loves you that much.

So find in your schedule a moment to be
A love to a stranger, love to the sea,
Love with the power my Jesus is to thee.

Your Mother of Peace and Love

...Be peace to this world,
Be love, not this war...

My presence thou gleaming,
My tears thus are streaming.
Be peace to this world,
Be love, not this war.

My hands thou are grasping,
To those who are lasting.
Be prayer to this world,
Be love, not this war.

My children, I'm calling,
Though my Son I'm stalling.
Be love in this world,
Be love, not this war.

Your help, yes, I'm asking,
It's strength, need you acting.
Be sure in this world,
Of the love, not the war.

I plead your forgiveness,
Your strong perseverance.
Be one in this world,
Be children of peace.

My presence thou waiting,
Must close soon, I'm stating.
Be peace to this world,
Be love, not this war.

To thee I shall visit,
Along His Sweet Spirit,
To gather my ones of peace,
Those of love, not of war.

Your Loving Gospa

...Come Holy Spirit, find my children near...

Come Holy Spirit, my children are near.
Remove their uncertainty, take away fear.
Bring up their spirits, embraced with Your love.
Make them an instrument, soaring as a dove.

Prepare their sweet spirits, so sweetness will win,
This battle We're fighting against evil and sin.
The shield You bestow will carry them through.
This love they invoke will give praise to You.

The vision of light, be clear, it's the path,
To protect and to guide away from the wrath.
So signal each heart, let Your Spirit thus be,
Within each one's soul, this Trinity.

Come Holy Spirit, find my children near.
Certain they are, there's no more fear.
Their spirits are lifted, embraced they must be.
The dove's soaring high, the Father, Son, and Thee.

Your Spirit's within, Your power they see,
Not eyes do they use, but vision indeed.
My mantle I wrap, to hold them all too,
So your Sweet Holy Spirit will reside anew.

My child of glory take up this grace.
Open your hearts to this spirited place.
Know We protect you, even unseen.
Know We're the sight of a pure heart's true gleam.
Let this pure heart be your heart, your means.

Your Mother of Love
Peace to my people, Peace

...I stand beside you, as a ray from the Son...

My child, I walk through all of the valleys with you.
My Son sent me to protect and give guidance too.
With consecration, I do not leave you at all.
Say but a word, I'll answer your call.

I stand beside you, as a ray from the Son.
My hope, to bring to His temple, all as one.
Before His eyes you must stand, it is true.
This just Judge is awaiting, can't you?

See the signs of this season thus change.
Know your prayers aren't extending the rain.
Be the light, connected to Thee.
Be a ray, choose His light, be standing by me.

Your Mother of Love

...Embrace the faith He sent you,
find Him in the night...

With my mantle wrapped around you, you would think they'd see
  the truth.
Yet so many flee its presence, that the flock We have is few.
They deny eternal life by their souls today not living.
They rely on coins and honey for their satisfaction—not the giving.

My little one, that which my Son divides is now.
Find your place, take your refuge. Let your heads then take a bow.
Await in peace, my loved ones, as the clouds rush by so white.
Embrace the faith He sent you, find Him in the night.

Employ the works He's asking, take in those not so pure.
For the refuge that you offer is a place that is secure.
No light can show the story, so brightly waiting thee.
Take hold of all that's holy—embrace His Trinity.

Gospa—Queen of Peace

...I lifted with glory—Our souls did not part...

My faith in knowing that I'd again see my Son,
Brought me into the light, brought Us as One.
For in believing in God, the pain of my heart,
I lifted with glory—Our souls did not part.

Take oh thy pains, give it to Him, I plead.
He's the answer to prayer, the love that you need.
Impress on your souls, this willingness to be,
Not a prisoner still, but a soul next to Thee.

What suffering now must be, shorter or long,
To my Son, please flee, His heart you belong.
So, faith in your being must reign, so it's true.
This faith that brings hope, from my Son's love to you.

Your Mother of Love

...My children, I bring love to you,
as a drop of dew brings warmth to a flower—
so that you are wrapped with this heavenly presence.

My love, seek such purity, love with such life,
As the grace of existence brings glory to strife.
Abate that so lonely, as foliage with no sun.
Bring light to your soul. Be Trinity's son.

Bring peace to your presence, in your cup so high.
To you does He send, glory this night.
Prepare only that which shines through the day.
His saving grace, will bring you Our way.

Your love fulfilled,
Your Mother,
Your Gospa

...Seek to know my Son's Divine Love...

I sing a melody of flowers and fine wine,
Bringing the fruit, giving the vine.
Reach for this gift of harmony sweet.
Touch of the presence, graced by His feet.

Bestow all you can from the gifts that I bring.
This music only heard from hearts that can sing.
Encourage the lost, scurry quickly my friends.
Time passes quickly, vines have their ends.

Partake of such glory, by taking that We give.
Choose of the fruit of life, so to live.
Behold to the faith, bow down your sweet head.
Trust in His presence, know why He bled.

My loved ones grow fuller with grace from above.
Seek to know my Son's Divine Love.
Take on to this melody, the vine you must cling.
For my Son's Heart is open and with glory you'll sing.
My Son's arms are open—to Thee I shall bring.

Your Loving Mother

...I carry the work of a mother in arms...

My children of grace, today I come to you in pink.
It's the color of faith; it's the heart's sweet tinct.
I carry the work of a mother in arms,
Her faithful patience, her smile, her charms.

I bring her the garden of strength that she needs,
To tolerate life, to give and to please.
I hold on to her duties as she takes one at a time,
And when she juggles them all, I help her do fine.

I know of her love for her children so dear,
I gave her my feelings, the ones with a tear.
I know that she listens and wants only the best,
For those that she's nurtured, those that take of her rest.

Endure, my mothers, my loved ones so pure.
Your duties I'm guiding; your children I cure.
The angels are swarming beside them at night.
They're keeping them holy and in God's great light.

So mothers, withstand all the jobs you must keep.
I'm standing beside you, you'll conquer defeat.
I'm holding your worries, I'm holding your hands too.
Embrace all with glory, my love, I'm with you.

Your Loving Mother

...Hearts of warmth enkindle such flame, that can grow to the Great Fire of Love...

Of choice and of will,
Of mountain, of hill,
Behold that within.
Remove that of sin.

Flourished all with fire from His heavenly crown,
The glory, the flame, the presence that's found.
My children of wonder, my children of truth,
Hold out that embrace, that heart of such youth.

And engulfed with His fire, ever within brows of Grace—
The presence within you will surpass that of taste,
Surpassing emotion, impounding your senses, resounding
    this grace.
The presence you find, yourself joining through,
Will be His Sweet Spirit, His Heart within you.

Your Loving Mother

...May you touch His ever presence,
May you hold on to His hem...

May the peace of love surround you,
As you walk amid such fear.
May you know We stand beside you.
When you feel so far, We're near.

May your days ahead be holy,
And the nights not bring you dark.
May the sound within your thunder,
Be of song, and ever lark.

May you see the face of God,
Amid the misty life so dim.
May you touch His ever presence,
May you hold on to His hem.

He awaits you; He longs for each of you.
Choose this love, today, I plead.
My children, I love you.
My children, my seeds.

Your Loving Mother

...You are called because my Son needs you to be His "Soldiers of the Trinity"...

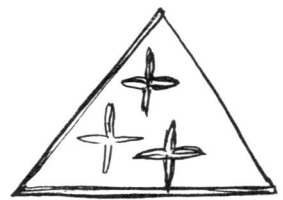

Hold not back that which was gifted by grace.
Stand forward with strength, stand firm in your place.
I lead you so kindly, your shoulders so bold.
My Trinity's Fire in your hearts you will hold.

Your Gospa of Love

...Those in the light,
marked with this blood, will be
ever enkindled in the Fire of His Love...

Find comfort in prayer, my valley awaits.
The ocean is roaring, my Son thus egates.

My children, I love you, my tears, they are red.
The hearts not of God bring thorns to His head.

Those in the light, marked with this blood,
Will be ever enkindled in the Fire of His Love.

Your Mother of Love

...Priestly people you must be,
to carry out His solemn plea...

Priestly people you must be,
To carry out His solemn plea.

He needs you soldiers, needs your prayer.
He's asking this in His despair.

Bring up your weapons—your breastplate of love.
Take on the challenge, this life's firm glove.

In prayer and fast, you'll be that to Thee,
His army of love, His nation complete.

Prepare thou souls, each brings new light.
Be willing to choose Him, in view of the fight.

Be bold in your faith, this battle's only begun.
The fear is surmounting. You are the one.

Persevere my children, don't give in to this war.
Be the soldier who wins. Be His bright shining star.

Your Most Loving Mother—Gospa

...Be awake my loving children,
Be the light upon the gate...

As you prepare your tables,
Await in prayer my friends;
My Son has raised His hand.
Thee you must defend.

Find love in each day given,
Find peace to thee within.
Be certain of your standing;
Know my Son is to begin.

Invoke the prayer He's asking,
In the silence of your thoughts.
It's the intimacy He's asking.
It's the words, no lips befall.

Choose this life, the glory waiting.
Choose the peace, We ask you take.
Be His vessel ever sailing,
Be His light, from darkness wake.

Carry out thy faithful duties,
Ever mindful of this wait.
Be awake my loving children,
Be the light upon the gate.

Your Loving Mother

...Find faith, hope, and love
at your doorstep of life...

The peace you must be is the way you find Thee,
Flowing the river, searching the sea.

The arrow of night that guides one so true,
The signal so blue, like a diamond in hue.

Find faith, hope, and love at your doorstep of life.
It's the table of plenty, the table of life.

May your guidance so pure,
Bring my Son to your cure.

Be His soldier by day.
Be His presence every way.

As you sing of His praises,
In all of your phrases,

Flow the river so blue,
And the sea—Thee to you.

Your Gospa of Love

...Set your souls free to be all you can be...

My children, thank you for listening to my words of plea.
I pray you enact now with bent knee.
I bring you the rainbow, He sends you the ray.
I lead you so kindly, He asks you to stay.

Be not afraid, for the place We thus set,
Is a garden of glory, a home you've not met.
Take hold of your purpose, pursue it with vigor too.
Within this mantle, you are wrapped all in blue.

Be the imitation of Thee, be His freedom in Three.
Set your souls free to be all you can be.
Set your souls free.
Be His, be of Thee.

Gospa of Love

...Bring the whiteness within you,
the same sweet within, as the
lilies I'm picking to take away sin...

I bring you the lilies, so white from above,
The fragrance of love, the song of the dove.
Embellish such flavor within thy sweet soul.
Be the bearer of plenty, the heart filled with gold.

This purity within, that I bring, please do take.
Have the courage and desire, the care to partake.
Bring the whiteness within you, the same sweet within,
As the lilies I'm picking to take away sin.

Though the choices aren't simple that come to your way,
The choice of Our Father is the choice of today.
And the soul that partakes with this cleansing and hope,
Is the soldier He's choosing, the stem and the yoke.

So take of these flowers, bring them close to your heart.
It's the place of the cleansing, the place you must start.
And even the purist can be whiter than these.
Be the bearer of fruit to the Father, and please.
Be all that they stand for, with prayer on thy knees.

Your Loving Mother

...Examine thy soul, bring it up to His cup...

I lead to thy Son, it's where you must go.
Follow closely my children, let your hearts grow.
Within His Sweet Spirit, you'll sing of great joy.
I give you My King, this prize of my boy.

Sing of His stories, His place in your heart,
Each morning of glory is a beginning, a start.
To love and to live, in His light from on High,
To be from example, the word and the life.

Examine thy soul, bring it up to His cup.
Immerse it in heaven, let Him lift thy soul up.
Protect and be humble, my Son loves you so.
Be His bright shining star, be His moon with a glow.

Your Loving Mother

...Let words and ways speak holiness,
and surround you with His sweet caress...

Prepare the way for Our Lord,
He is here to set you free.
May the river take you quickly
To the place He's set for thee.

Be ever at His side each day,
At morn and again at night.
The path He's taking you through, My child,
Is one within His flight.

Combine the dream—thought elements,
Of love, trust, peace, in one, as well.
Examine, yet be proud of thee,
And meek within thy cell.

For glory does thou wait for those,
Who shape their hearts to thus—your task,
A splendor of a soul, my one,
A joining of that He asks.

So speak the words He longs to hear,
And words within thou holiness.
Prayer be your life, from dawn to dusk,
Will bring His presence, and you He'll bless.

Let words and ways speak holiness,
And surround you with His sweet caress.

Your Loving Mother

...And the treasure you've worked for,
within you shall be, the gold-ribbon
name of my Son within thee...

Jesus

Look not at the shadows in your life,
The what went wrong,
But the soul you're perfecting,
The angel's song.

Look not to the riches
You didn't gain,
But within, to the riches
You earned through pain.

My children, take graces
That He's sending your way.
They're here for protection,
Here to stay.

When passing through struggles,
You always ask why.
Just lift up your chin
And take a great sigh.

For the soul that does live
For God's will, each new day,
Brings graces within Him,
Sanctity remains.

And the treasure you've worked for
Within you shall be,
The gold-ribbon name
Of my Son within thee.

And the treasure you bring
To His throne in the end will be
Welcomed, those He created,
Those you received.

                    Your Gospa of Love

...Only the <u>light of love</u> is the True Light...

Praise and glory to my Son—
Await His power, await the One.
Find truth within you; this warning I give—
His purging of souls, will choose those who live.

Your Mother of Love

...For only the faithful, those loving with <u>His</u> Heart, will become one with Him, join His eternal depart...

How many sunsets must they see to believe,
Of this miracle of life that was given to thee?

How many rainbows must you see in this sky,
To know of His homeland, that awaits you up high?

My voice does grow silent with each solemn plea.
Turn thy hearts now to gold; Get down on thy knee.

For only the faithful, those loving with <u>His</u> Heart,
Will become one with Him, join His eternal depart.

So bow down your heads, do His work, while you may,
For the time for His glory—the time for His song will be any day.
For the time of His glory can be yours if you pray.

Your Loving Mother

...Be not afraid, I send you Peace,
Faith, the Rosary, the Scapular, and Love...

It is good and just to serve our King,
From evening star to morning's ring.   **Peace**
From East to West, I travel far,
To bring you peace, to plead thus far.

My merry children of great faith's stand,
It's in your hands, it's in your land.   **Faith**
Bow down thy heads, speak of Him on high.
Show only love, not angry pride.

Stay closely to those tools I sent,
The rosary near, it's grace intent.   **The Rosary**
For slowly now, thy soldiers come,
To be with Thee, to hold the One.

Upon thy breast, this plate I gave thee,
Will bring thee showers of grace, you'll see. **The Scapular**
So wear it proudly, protection of true.
My Son sees your face, surrounded by blue.

My Son sees your soul in its love-filled hue.   **Love**

Your Loving Gospa

...So breathe His Sweet Spirit— let zeal set your sail...

The face that shines with peace so true,
Must be my soldier with armor anew.
That dusty shelf within, thus cleaned,
Those panes that fogged, now shine with gleam.

Go deeper to seek what my Son calls you to,
The shadows removed, and the soul you renew.
Go further than ever, the prize is set high,
The castle that's waiting, above His blue sky.

And reaching this destiny, though never quite there,
The further thy travels, the clearer the air.
So breathe His Sweet Spirit—let zeal set your sail.
Take hold to thy journey, leave love as thy trail.
Take hold, my dear children, let your peace take your sail.

Your Gospa of Love

...Child of great mercy,
I hand you the chain...

Child of great mercy, I hand you the chain.
Take on this lead, to take away His pain.

Praise be your melody, love be the song.
My Son is thus waiting, His waiting's so long.

Ignite thy sweet spirit with His love from above,
If His glory you live, you'll soar like the dove.

In humble desire, He thus whispers your name.
Let your soul to Thee rise, let your love be the same.

May this union be true, for His love thus He shares.
May you bring with thy flock, your sweet love and your cares.

Take hold to the mission, not this life's, but my Son's.
Be the fire of His love, each one then becomes.

Write your name in His Heart, Stay within my loved one.
Join the Father, His Spirit, join the soul of my Son.

Your Loving Mother

...Come to the altar of love,
embrace His sweet gift...

Come to the water of Sanctity and Grace.
He sees of your love and desires.
He looks at your face.

Come to the altar of love, embrace His sweet gift.
Take away pain within His Heart.
Let your heart lift.

Bar not the faith that's wanting to live,
In a heart turned to gold,
From the love you did give.

Come to the mountain, waiting kindly beside me.
Bring only that worthy
To present then to Thee.

And as we thus wait for His return— through the night,
You'll feel His fine glory,
You'll taste of His might.

And as we thus wait His return— break of day,
You'll live in His shadow,
To become in His way.

For the shadow of my Son is a rainbow of love.
Sanctity from above,
His hand in your glove.

The shadow, not of darkness, but light from on high,
The peace thus unfolding, love felt from His sigh.
The love thus unfolded from His sign in the sky.

Your Loving Mother

...I speak to you this day in a plea for prayer...

Rejoice in the glory, my Son lifts His hand.
The waters are raging and the desperate seek land.
Take hold of thy faith, it's the gift worth in gold.
Take hold, you must love, you must fight and be bold.

The choices won't be written with answers exact.
Divine intervention is the grace, not to lack.
For in making these choices, those without sin.
You'll need God in your soul, just to breathe Him within.

My children, it's urgent, this peace, prayer, and love.
Be certain you visit my Son up above.
Be certain your door in your heart stays open to Him.
The will you must choose is of Him, not of sin.

Your Loving Mother

...Open arms and palms,
take His cross, hold it close...

Today I arrive with a cross in my hand.
To show of the pain my Son suffers across this land.
Open arms and palms, take His cross, hold it close.
It's your welcome of love, a sign He'll expose.

All you give to my child, I return to thee so free.
Breathe His Sweet Breath, let your wisdom be of Thee.
As you cleanse thy soul, imperfections still arise—
Take hold, be of mercy, be of Sanctity's comprise.

Continue thy journey, We stand by your side.
Belong to my family of Faith—Love, not pride.
Be whole from within, yes the touch of His song,
Will be flowing within you, to Thee you'll belong.

Mother of Mercy

...Examine, be patient, be true to His love...

I come to you with the splendor of heaven around my gown.
I bring you this presence, as a gift—faith has found.
Partake of these gifts, while the grace thus does flow,
My Son will be with thee when through darkness you go.

What then will thee have as tools and as color?
Only the faith as your rainbow within to bring light fuller.
Only flowers of love within will thee see,
For this world that you know will long to be free.

Examine, be patient, be true to His love.
Hold the graces We've brought you in a treasure from above.
For within is the "all" you will be in the end.
A sweet spirit that's soaring, the soul open to Him.
A sweet spirit presented to my Son's flowing hem.

Your Loving Mother
Queen of Peace

...I bring you the blossoms
when nothing will grow,
in the darkness of night,
in a field cold with snow...

I sing of the songs you have not yet heard ring.
The words from afar, the melody of spring.
I send you the birds, their flight through the storm—
This life decomposing and taking new form.

I bring you the blossoms when nothing will grow,
In the darkness of night, in a field cold with snow.
Into such warmth will you find this mantle thus gives,
To those marked by my Son, those choosing to live.

Be certain of peace and a cleansing through pain,
Be sure that your faith, in my Son thus remains.
I bring you protection, don't flee, but stay near.
His judgment is coming, keep Us close, keep Us near.

Your Mother of Love and Mercy

...From Our Lady of Grace...

The grace of the wind that sings a sweet song,
Is waiting to greet thee, to make thee belong.

The grace of the sun that shines down His love,
Is waiting to warm thee, to make thee belong.

The grace of the rain that cleanses with peace,
Is waiting to wash thee, to make thee belong.

The grace you find present when darkness follows closely,
Brings peace and true love to the heart that belongs.

The grace of perseverance that becomes your blanket of love,
Will be yours for belonging to His kingdom above.

Your Mother of Love

...In thanksgiving, do as my Son asks,
as He must change the world from each present
existence, and He needs your help to do so...

He wants love from His soldiers,
That in armor there they stand.
He wants faith beyond mountains;
Judging not found in this land.

He wants peace in your hearts;
There's no room for discordance or beyond.
Only want of thy soul's place,
Beside Him found.

The break of dawn shall greet you,
And above you'll see His sign.
Those who say tomorrow isn't here,
I must remind.

There is no time for rushing to His feet, only in the end.
You must be there today,
My ones, be there and do pray.
Be there, and do please pray.

Your Mother of Love

...Be the soar of the Spirit, be at peace, be of love...

I stand beside my Son with great mercy and love.
He's sent you His Spirit—with the sign of the dove.

He brings thus His presence to each that desires.
Be faith, hope, and love, be of happiness and wise.

Not fear in your hearts, but filled with desire,
He'll replace it with His Spirit—the Man you admire.

He'll make your soul dance with the touch of His song.
It's the Trinity's Sweet Spirit, that will wisp you along.

Be precious to the King, be His soldier, be His child.
He's been standing next to thee, hand in hand all the while.

Lighten my burden for the hope of these souls,
I find the Spirit's not received by so many, not their goal.

Open thy wings, become part of the dove,
Be the soar of the Spirit, be at peace, be of love.

Your Mother Above

...I bring you through blue,
it's the Trinity's hue...

I bring you through blue, it's Trinity's hue,
For the prisms of white, bring blue back to you.
I wrap you with kindness, please take it within.
Bring peace to Our people, and all that's for Him.

Can you answer yes to a question once asked?
Will you be One with the King? Will you find love sur-
passed?
Will you risk all you know just to show Him you care?
Will you bring Him the flowers, leaving them bare?

For with faith they will grow, not needing life's soil.
They will blossom so plenty—the heart's yes is the toil.
Be sure of thy answer, it's right there in you—
It's the longing for union, that will lead you to blue.

Your Lady in Blue

...For in all, we are the same,
to live His Holy Name...

I await the star of night,
That brought my Son to life.
Though cold and pain presided,
I had the strength beside me.

May the days ahead bring glory.
Each one to find their story.
For in all, we are the same,
To live His Holy Name.

The peace and joy will bring thee
To stables filled with His glee.
For although His birth was then,
Today, is it again.

The birth within thy soul,
The season that is told,
Prepares and brings thus forth
The heart that He thus courts.

And as you seek to know
Of the love that brought me so,
You'll see within thy soul
The glory that unfolds.

The birth within thy soul
Of my Son—the story told.
The birth within, that longs
To be—Our Lord—belongs.

So at this time reflect,
And allow the leap of respect
For the King, thus born within,
And the song you'll sing of Him.

Your Mother of Love

...My Son sends these angels
to you to behold...

Angels fly by night and day,
Protecting you each moment you pray.

They send down a presence, so precious and sweet.
They'll lift up your spirit in the day's long retreat.

Be certain my loved ones, with me do they sing.
Not the hark of a coldness, but the harkening of spring.

And as the wind sings with a melody untold,
My Son sends these angels to you to behold,

Of the coming of the Savior, the coming of my Son,
From the Father's House to your place in the sun.

Your Loving Mother

...Let these leaves that are
brown—in your heart—turn to gold...

The leaves of faith that fall from His tree
Are bringing such peace, for all to see.
Bring them closely my love, bring them into thy soul.
Let these leaves that are brown—in your heart—turn to gold.

Your Mother of Love

...The more you behold Him,
the more you will gain...

Catch the tear of the morning.
Catch its gleam from the sun.
Be awakened by beauty,
From the soul and my Son.

Arise thus in day
With the touch of His love.
Be the beacon that rises.
Be the faith's only glove.

And as your day advances,
Think of many a time
That my Son walked to live
So that we could walk in time.

Be brave as you're carried.
You're escorted through life.
Give Him, the Director,
Your Guide, give Him the prize.

Your heart full of love,
Full of freedom from pain,
For the more you behold Him,
The more you will gain.

Your Mother of Peace and Love

...My children, your journeys
are blessed from above...

The wind, how it blows; Can you tell its direction?
Your prayer, though it glows must peak its perfection.

Be humbled to silence, about you'll find peace.
Be ready for rapids, as waters thus seek.

My children, your journeys are blessed from above.
You're seeking to continue, my Son leads with love.

Bring prayer in your heart, let it flow with such love.
And the peace that We send will whistle from above,
Like a wind that's inflamed by the Fire of His Love.

Your Loving Gospa
Queen of Peace

...Whisper words of wisdom, from the echo that you hear...

Whisper words of wisdom,
From each echo that you hear.
The words He gives so freely,
To the blessed heart so dear.

Take this grace and use it,
For it's given on this day.
A simple quest of purity,
The love you gain and pray.

Explain the simple yearnings,
From the hearts that reach for more,
And fill them with His Spirit,
As you grace them—love that pours.

In viewing that which finds you
At the foot of heaven's door,
You long that same sweet spirit
That guides you ever more.

So praise His name in scripture,
Find His face in those you meet.
Be the flame He has still burning.
Be His song, and be complete.

Your Loving Mother

...Take the steps of Our Father,
let Him guide and remake...

I come as the Queen of Peace, my child.
I see of your sorrows, I want you to smile.
My presence so peaceful will flourish within.
This mission He's asking will help remove sin.

Be ready, my loved one, new journeys begin.
Take away old that has weighted within.
Be that by His side as you walk in such peace.
Feel the love your heart glides as your worries thus cease.

With winter of staleness, to spring thus of change,
You'll feel of the prayer in your lives rearranged.
You'll seek, that's the key, to this journey you take.
Take the steps of Our Father, let Him guide and remake.

My children, sing praise, for He's wanting you so
To be all you can be, empty out, and then grow.
By the task that you follow, the destiny of love,
You'll be molded and folded in the palm of His glove.

Peace, my children. Prayer.
Your Mother—Queen of Peace

**...So raise thine eyes,
turn your face to my Son...**

From the barren branches that rest this day,
You'll take the walk to a brighter way.
You'll give to the change, Our King desires,
And when the spring is here, you'll be Ours.

This span of time, of fast and peace,
Will be your desert of life to beat.
You'll see temptation, face life's demands.
The struggle of people, the Lord by—He stands.

But perseverance, my child, it's the faith into act.
It's the way you believe when life gives nothing back.
It's the slumbering life when you think it should be,
Awake in God's love, alive just as He.

So faith turned to gold, nothing new, just as told
Is the way you walk placidly through to your goal.
For in seeking His truth, you're climbing those heights,
And by desiring His valley, you'll be that of might.

So raise thine eyes, <u>turn your face to my Son</u>.
He's the glorious incarnate who became one
With the Trinity of Love, the Holiest of all,
Our God, Our Father, Your Spirit to call.

Intrigued by the beauty of heaven's great light,
The Trinity sends as part of its flight
To the soul that is seeking, being present within,
To the Kingdom, its glory, and the God you defend.

During this span of days looking gloom,
Those branches so barren, will suddenly bloom.
The dryness of persistence, when nothing took you there,
Becomes tranquil with color, and thy thirst becomes scarce.

The presence within you that kept you in Him,
Was the face in the sun that today isn't dim.
Then walk from this barren to the waters of life,
That will greet you and raise you to God's place up high—
Raise you and praise you for the strength and the might.

Your Loving Mother

...The presence of holiness, about to embark within, as a candle is lit in the dark...

The presence of peace about you they'll see.
The way you express God's love to thee.
The presence of love will follow thee so,
Wherever you pray, wherever you go.

The presence of happiness that follows such love
Will embrace thee and chase thee, all from above.
The presence of joy will entangle these virtues
To bring giving and kindness and silence about you.

The presence of holiness, about to embark
Within, as a candle is lit in the dark.
The presence of my Son within you will be
The candle within, the absence of sin,
And the grace of a life filled with His Trinity.

Embracing you with love so true,
Your Loving Mother Crowned in Blue

...A treasure of presence,
immersed in His name...

We stand before you, a beacon of light,
To bring forth such glory, to give you insight.

To lead you to others, searching for the truth,
To bring them back home to the place of their youth.

We touch you with graces, with the breath of the wind.
We're sending you out into the crowd full of sin.

We're hoping they feel the touch of Our love,
Traveling and following in the Spirit above.

It's time for my children to come back, turn around,
To the heart He's revealing, to the love that's profound.

It's time to change from the lacking of faith
To a mountain, not to stumble, as thy walk takes you straight.

Envelop such love, for join hands with the King.
Say, my Father, I love Thee and have mercy on me.

Take off into flight, no fear, only peace.
For I shower thee with blue and graces won't cease.

I take thee right through and His power remains.
And the presence you feel is the elevation from pain,
A treasure of presence, immersed in His name.

Your Loving Mother

Prayer Given For Discernment

Jesus, in Your Heart I reside,
Your most Holy Spirit protect and guide.

With divine presence,
Your Most Loving Father